WALKING

WITH THE

DIVINE

Poems of

Love and Devotion

By

Omer Toledano

~

Dedicated to the Dedicated

Devoted to the Devoted

With Love to the Beloved

~

The Water Knows

By

Omer Toledano

When you're there in the water

It's a fresh cool sensation

It cleans you of all

Removes condensation

In this liquid you're free

It's all relaxation

You're stripped of your worries

You feel some elation

It's you and the water

And your inhalation

It's you and the water
It's you blowing bubbles
Exhaling the air
Releasing your troubles
To be there in water
Is a natural thing
You can mumble and curse
Or just start to sing

It knows who you are
It knows how you feel
It tells you right now
It shows you it's real
There's magic in water
It is no illusion
Your body submerged
In this clear solution
It sings all around you
With glimmers of light
It is meditation
It's sight beyond sight

You feel quite reborn
In this pool of water
When it's cold at the start
And then becomes hotter
The water remembers
You were there once before
You were there many times
It knows to keep score

It speaks what you feel
If you're gentle or kind
If you're rough on the edges
Or of clear lucid mind
If the liquid is tough
If you cut through like butter
So much can be learned
While swimming in water

~

The Realm of the Faceless

By

Omer Toledano

One day I will wake up

I will wake up from this dream

And see your true face

Your true nature

One day I will shed this mortal coil

This mortal toil

And then I will come to know

Your true being

I know who you are

You have always been there

The spinning globe

The sun rising in the east

Life sings its song

And You are here

With a blast of your nostrils

You move mountains

Please remove the veil

There is nothing left for me here

The Jig is up

I am close

Take my hand and pull me up

Sit me among the sea

Of forgotten souls

Let me look upon thy face

Let me look away

In the realm of the faceless

~

Infinity Code

By

Omer Toledano

It began with the light

So that we all could see

Him in the self

And you in the me

It started off clean

What was

Was what is

And continued and grew

What is mine is now his

The fruit from the trees

The honey from bees

Man is now ruler

Does whatever he please

Unless he does not

Go forth

Do some cleaning

He will never achieve

To understand the true meaning

He has lost his direction

He must make a correction

And cease to make splits

Into section and section

There is only one

There is no division

What he knows to be true

Has distorted his vision

This is his moment

A short time for laughter

For eternity spans there

Both before and then after

No use for attachment

It is all for rent

The house that you live in

Your car's side dent

And even your body

Will once wither away

And give room to another

And a brand new day

All you must do

Is remember that you

Are a part of the fabric

In all that you do

Who you see and you love

Is sent from above

To show you who you are

And what you are made of

Till we meet I give you

A blessing forever

A blessing for now

And a blessing for never

Please accept all that is

In this type of mode

And help me to write

My infinity code

~

Dance of Eternity

By

Omer Toledano

They've been dancing for years
Swaying for hours
Residing in silence
Presiding with powers
Clouds in formations
Rising of nations
Kings of the realm
Mad men at the helm
Up and down
And love comes to town
And then it comes closer
And off comes your gown

Then one day when you leave

I then sicken and heave

It then goes away

A storm, light of day

Consumed all by fire

And a loss of desire

It twists and then turns

Up in flames it burns

Delusions and visions

Human divisions

Physics in motion

Exchange of emotion

A heart beats in darkness

And the dark does not win

In the dance of eternity

You are out or you're in

~

The Magical Mule

By

Omer Toledano

The Magical Mule is one to behold
He is sharp, he is wise
He is strong and he's bold
The Magical Mule never gives up
He never surrenders
He is quite a chump
Day in and day out
He pulls his load
He treads alone
This lonely road
The Magical Mule cannot complain
If he's feeling ill
Or if he's in pain

It matters not

To his masters on Earth

The Magical Mule

Is both blessed and cursed

On the one hand he's blessed

For he's made a living

On the other he's cursed

No life and just giving

Who now weeps for this Magical Mule

Who has left this world

A shiny jewel

Who will care for this mule

In a hundred years' time

Who will remember his face

And know who he was

Just a Magical Mule

Who did not make a fuss

Who followed one rule

For he knows who he was

In every sense of the word

A Magical Mule

~

The Seed of Intention

By

Omer Toledano

There are things in this world

Beyond comprehension

Like time and its flow

With the seed of intention

You decide who you are

In each passing moment

What role do you play?

Is it joy or just torment?

Infinite wisdom is at our disposal

To reject all at once

Or accept a proposal

It's a game, simulation

Every choice that we make

Whether high in the air

Or enjoying a lake

Ultimate truth at the heart of creation

A place that is still

Where all comes to cessation

Perpetual movements

Of body and mind

Come to a halt

And there you will find

The answer to that

Which you have been asking

The ultimate truth

Which you have been masking

It was there all along

You were too blind to see

Too busy sailing

This stormy sea

Before leaving again
One more thing I should mention
Plant it here, plant it now
Your seed of intention

~

Autoresponse

By

Omer Toledano

The feeling is gone

I've lost the emotion

My current plea

A present notion

Maybe for the better

That I can no longer feel

That nothing has value

That it is no longer real

For others so simple

To trust

And cast meaning

So easy to fall

Against whom they are leaning

Time and again

It seems so obscure

All in its place

A magical cure

Like a program to start

To connect to the heart

To feel at the core

To open a door

Like a mouse in a lab

The yellow cab

Crosses the bridge

A metallic slab

A hotel in the city

A six year old boy

The world on his finger

To love and enjoy

I guess that is it
All that there is
Fading memories
Of all that is His
It is always the now
In all that was once
An empty reaction
An auto-response

~

Equinox

By

Omer Toledano

Something to be said

About this fluctuation

Twice a year it occurs

In our Earthly rotation

Once in the Autumn

And once in the Spring

Masculine Feminine

It's a beautiful thing

It is not felt by many

They're not even aware

Do not know it exists

Do not know it is there

North and South become one

And the sun is aligned

Equal light to the poles

It's a wonderful ride

Male turns to Female

Female turns to Male

Complete equilibrium

In this solar sail

The Earth keeps on spinning

In a slight slanted axis

And we to new worlds

Begin to gain access

Once we are there

Once we are here

It all lasts for cycles

Of half a year

It goes on through the ages

Felt by Scientists and Sages

It spins like a quarter

Maintains cosmic order

Shows to us all

That space has no border

To the firm disbeliever

Who reads this and mocks

Whether you know it or not

It is now equinox

~

Heartbeats & Seconds

By

Omer Toledano

The countdown begins

Refuse to bins

Throw the garbage away

And then second hand

Like grains of the sand

And the heart is trying to say

Heartbeat and second

Are in sync the boy reckoned

A purpose for every event

When time began

With a beat of his heart

And the motion to eternity sent

The world created with this vibration
It is sometimes well overlooked
For the rays of the sun
In his morning run
With the world this one is now hooked
Connected to all with umbilical cord
Which has never for once been severed
He is the Earth and the Sun and the Moon
A Nomad out in the desert
The air he breathes in and the blood in his veins
Constructions, a weak explanation
For they matter not in this house of delights
And they surely pose no limitation
Seduction of spirit is all there is here
And the mind is trying to bind you
With a backdrop for life
A flute and a fife
Look ahead and not what's behind you

A heartbeat a second

"Come with me!" the boy beckoned

What more evidence do you require?

I will carry your burden and ease your pain

Let me be your formidable squire

Where we go from here

In your hands it will be

As it has been right from the start

The hours and seconds will continue to pass

With the beating of your loving heart

~

In Memoriam

By

Omer Toledano

Please remember

That I was once your son

That once I filled your world

With wonder and delight

That once I was the center

That once I was alright

Please remember

That once I was your brother

Aggressive when I must

And only because once

In you I could not trust

Please remember

That I was once your friend

I saw myself in you

And you o' friend of mine

Saw the best in me

And let my spirit shine

Please remember

That I was once your lover

You showed me

What it means to love

To lose myself there in another

And you

Will you remember who you were

When all of this is gone

Will you remember anything

When all of this is done

Please remember everything

There is no good or bad

Your light shines to eternity

And nothing you once had

Nothing to take with you

No meat, no skin, no bone

For when time comes and comes to pass

To there you go alone

No memory of anything

Of you who is no more

It was all a test I put you through

To guide you to the door

Rest in peace o' child of mine

While walking through a garden

And know that you are here with me

Alone but not forgotten

~

The Servant

By

Omer Toledano

Leave me to dwell in your presence, divine one

Embrace me with your silence and eternal wisdom

Let me see through your eyes

The timeless melody of your unbounded song

Free me once more from this web of deception

So that I may once more empty myself of this deluge of
delusion

And find your path through the storm

Which you in your infinite wisdom

Have manifested with your mighty hand

To keep me from seeing the true intention of your
divine will

Find me once more o' great one

You know where I am

In purity will you come to know my intention

In beauty will you come to know my everlasting love

In truth will you come to know my way

There is no other

We are one

Your heart's echoing cry has brought me to you

once again

And there I shall remain

Your servant

For all eternity

~

Shadow

By

Omer Toledano

A wintry night

Black & mysterious

Cold & damp

Kid you not

I am serious

Whispering winds

Telling tales of long past

Floods and showers

How long will they last?

Sing me a song

Young maiden in yellow

Know me to sleep

Kiss this young-looking fellow

Where have they gone

Those sirens of old?

Why must I stand here out in the cold?

Come here young lady

To have and to hold

Till death do us part

On mountains of gold

This is my shadow

It is him so I'm told

Stand up straight

Stand up tall

Stand up strong

Stand up bold

Why must you stand there

You there in the back

Where is your light

That you desperately lack

What is your purpose

Who do you serve

Do you reap what you sow

And what you deserve

You are my shadow

You are me in the dark

If I was a fish

Why then you'd be a shark

We are one in the same

And we constantly fight

You in the dark

And me in the light

~

Made in the USA
Coppell, TX
13 January 2024

27569201R00023